WRITE ABOUT IT

Middle Grades

by Imogene Forte

Incentive Publications, Inc.   Nashville, Tennessee

Thank You

to Mary Catherine Mahoney

and to Susan Oglander

editors

to Becky Cutler

cover designer

and to Mary Hamilton

artist

ISBN 0-86530-046-1

These Adventures in Writing Belong to

_____

TABLE OF CONTENTS

WRITE ABOUT IT . . .

Ideas for Young Writers

- Look for new words in every book you read.
- Learn to spell one new w[...] every day.
- Write to a pen pal.
- Keep a diary.
- Write a play.
- Make lists of words & phrases [...] at c[...] excitement, describe and demand attention.
- Daydream, and write down your dreams.

WRITE ABOUT IT was written to provide interesting, fun-filled activities to help boys and girls achieve writing independence. Each page has been carefully designed to reinforce and extend one or more writing skills. Easy-to-follow directions, fanciful contemporary-based themes, and the use of a controlled but not limited vocabulary encourage purposeful personal writing.

To simplify classroom or home use, the reproducible activity pages have been organized into two broad areas:

I. Vocabulary development and technical writing skills
   A. Parts of speech
   B. Word usage
   C. Word meanings
   D. Punctuation and capitalization
   E. Writing sentences and paragraphs

II. Composition and original writing
   A. Organizing ideas
   B. Special literary devices
   C. Prose and poetry

Each of the worksheets is designed to stand alone and provide one complete writing experience. They may be used to supplement and reinforce adopted courses of study and are appropriate for use in individual or group settings. For classroom use, teachers will want to review the skills as listed in the table of contents and plan the order and manner of presentation to meet student needs. In a home or other setting where the book is used individually, the pages will fall into a natural skills sequence and can be used most efficiently in the order presented.

The purposes of this collection of read-think-and-write activities are to encourage kids to stretch their minds, develop their imaginations, and enjoy the thrill of successful writing.

Get your pencil; WRITE ABOUT IT!

Imogene Forte

VOCABULARY DEVELOPMENT
and
TECHNICAL WRITING SKILLS

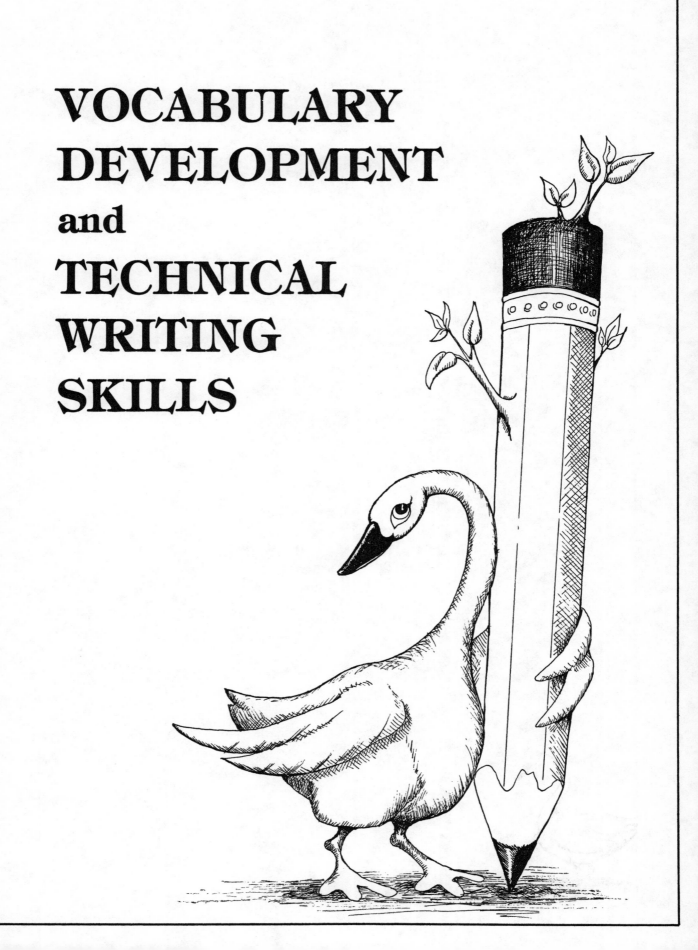

TIME TO WRITE

Professional writers say that the best way to become a really good writer is to write, write, write.

Begin your writing record today.

Set a time limit for completing the record.

_____ 's Writing Record

(your name)

Things To Write	Title or Comment	Date
Ad		
Autobiography		
Biography		
Cartoon		
Editorial		
Fable		
Greeting card		
Jokes		
Letter		
Memo		
Myth		
Note		
Novel		
Play		
Poetry		
Recipe		
Riddles		
Slogan		
Speech		
Tall tale		

NOUNS, NOUNS, NOUNS!

A *noun* is the name of a person, place, or thing.

Select a topic that interests you right now. (Examples: space exploration, desert life, camping, scuba diving.)

Write as many nouns as you can think of that are related to the topic.

Try to use some unusual nouns.

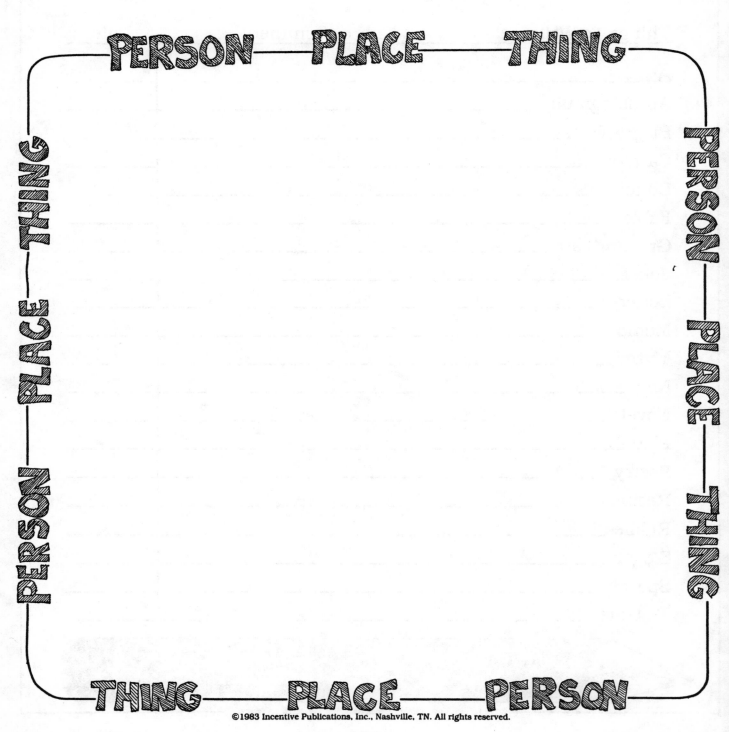

SUNDAE AFTERNOON

Adjectives are used to help readers see a person, place, or thing as the writer sees it. The writer of the story below used too many adjectives. Rewrite the story using fewer adjectives to make the story clearer and more interesting.

Pat decided one afternoon to make a big, giant, huge ice cream sundae. He opened the freezer and took out containers of 3 of his best-liked, favorite flavors. He put 2 large, oversized scoops of each into a clear, crystal, glass bowl. Then he poured sweet, sugary, syrupy chocolate sauce on top of it. He added billowy, fluffy whipped cream and some little, small pieces of chopped pecan. After topping his sundae with a luscious bright red cherry, Pat was ready to eat. He had created a delicious-looking, scrumptious-tasting sundae, just as he had imagined.

_____

_____

_____

_____

_____

_____

_____

_____

_____

_____

_____

_____

_____

COLOR-A-CRITTER

Use crayons or felt tip pens to color the picture.
Write 10 words or phrases to describe the critter.
Use the words and phrases to write a story about your critter.

1. _____
2. _____
3. _____
4. _____
5. _____
6. _____
7. _____
8. _____
9. _____
10. _____

_____

_____

_____

_____

_____

_____

_____

_____

PATIENCE REWARDED

Underline the adverbs in the sentences below.
On the line below each sentence, write an adverb from the word list that can be used in place of the underlined word.

Word list:
frequently
soon
barely
positively
approximately
apparently
partially

1. Andy had often seen raccoons in the woods near his house, and he decided to observe a raccoon for his science project.

   _____

2. He had read that raccoons wash their food, and he knew he absolutely had to see it for himself.

   _____

3. After dinner one evening, Andy took some fruit and corn and walked to a spot roughly 15 feet inside the woods near a stream.

   _____

4. He placed the food beside the stream and moved behind a tree so he would be partly hidden.

   _____

5. He watched for half an hour, but seemingly it wasn't a good night to observe raccoons.

   _____

6. It was getting dark, and Andy could hardly see.

   _____

7. Presently, just as he was ready to give up, he heard a sound. It was his raccoon! The experiment was going to work after all!

   _____

COMPUTER COUNTDOWN

Take this quiz to find out if you are a real computer whiz.

Tell what part of speech each word in the sentences below is by writing the proper number from the computer code in each space.

Add up the numbers in each line and compare your total with the "computer total" at the end of each line.

Code:
Noun 1
Verb 2
Adjective 3
Adverb 4
Preposition 5
Conjunction . . . 6
Pronoun 7
Interjection 8

	Your total	Computer total
1. Here is a computer.		10
2. It can provide valuable information.		15
3. Have you ever used a computer?		19
4. Put the plug into the socket and turn the switch.		27
5. The computer will tell you how to operate it.		30
6. Can you read the printout?		15
7. Oh! Someone unplugged the computer!		21

TROLL TURNABOUT

In an old fairy tale, a princess turned a frog back into a prince just by kissing it. See if you can do the same for a poor prince who was turned into a troll by an evil sorcerer.

Read the paragraph below. Turn the troll into a prince by rewriting the paragraph. Use the correct antonym from the antonym tree for every underlined word.

Once there was a very <u>ugly</u> <u>troll</u>. He was <u>squat</u> and <u>dark</u> and had <u>short</u>, <u>dark</u>, <u>straight</u> hair. His clothes were of the <u>coarsest</u> <u>black</u> <u>cotton</u>, and his <u>old</u> <u>sandals</u> were made of <u>straw</u> and were <u>sloppily</u> sewn together. His hand was <u>weak</u>, and he often used his <u>dingy</u> <u>club</u> to do <u>bad</u> deeds. He was very <u>unhappy</u>, for everyone <u>hated</u> him. People <u>disliked</u> being around him because of his <u>mean</u> nature. He always had <u>cruel</u> things to say and tried to <u>hurt</u> people in trouble.

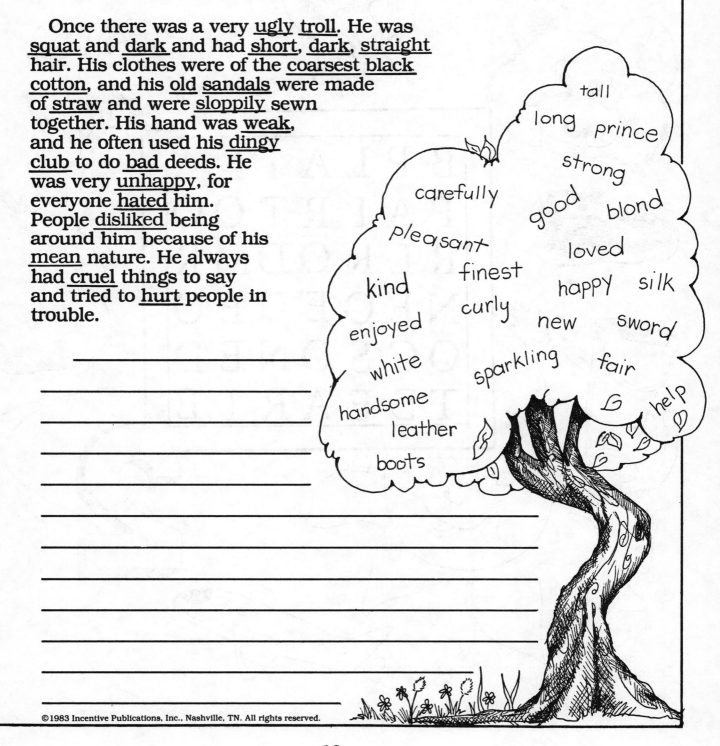

_____

_____

_____

_____

_____

_____

_____

_____

_____

_____

HOMONYM HUNT

A *homonym* is a word that is pronounced exactly like another word but is often spelled differently and always has a different meaning.

Find and circle a homonym in the word-find puzzle for each picture.

```
B P L A I N A
P A I R T O O
R L R O D M R
N E O E U E O
O C S O N E D
T D E A R T E
```

ROYAL POSSESSIONS

On the line under each picture, write a phrase that labels the picture.

Make the first word in each phrase show possession.

Then on the lines below, write a short story using the phrases.

(king, throne)

(queen, crown)

(princess, cloak)

(dog, fleas)

(beggar, rags)

(watchman, keys)

_____

_____

_____

_____

_____

_____

A VERY PRECISE LISTING

Ali Author has worked for a long time to become a good writer. Editors tell him that he needs to learn to be more precise.

Help Ali develop a list of precise synonyms for each of the overworked words on his list.

big (adjective)

1. _____
2. _____
3. _____
4. _____
5. _____
6. _____

good (adjective)

1. _____
2. _____
3. _____
4. _____
5. _____
6. _____

place (verb)

1. _____
2. _____
3. _____
4. _____
5. _____
6. _____

quickly (adverb)

1. _____
2. _____
3. _____
4. _____
5. _____
6. _____

get (verb)

1. _____
2. _____
3. _____
4. _____
5. _____
6. _____

Don't forget to use the more precise words in your own writing!

A RED-LETTER DAY

Careful writers avoid using expressions that have been worn out by too much use (such as the title of this page).

Underline 10 overworked expressions in the story below.

Then rewrite the story and substitute better words for the underlined phrases.

Molly was happy as a lark on Friday afternoon. She had been invited to spend the night with her friend Loretta, and her brother was going to drive her to Loretta's house. But getting there was easier said than done. The car battery was dead as a doornail. Molly ran next door and found a neighbor who was glad to lend a helping hand. At long last, Molly and her brother arrived at Loretta's house.

"Better late than never!" Loretta exclaimed. Molly's face lit up like a Christmas tree. There were all her friends with birthday gifts for her! To make a long story short, Molly had the time of her life at her first surprise party, and she arrived just in the nick of time.

_____

_____

_____

_____

_____

_____

_____

_____

_____

_____

_____

STRETCHING YOUR WORD POWER

Choose one of the following words. Then follow the directions for "stretching your word power."

buy   fair
night   new

Look up the meaning in your dictionary.

_____   _____
(word)   (meaning)

_____

Write the words which come before and after this word on the dictionary page.

_____   _____

Write words which rhyme with this word.

_____ _____ _____

_____ _____ _____

Write:

Synonyms	Antonyms	Homonym
1. _____	1. _____	1. _____
2. _____	2. _____	
3. _____	3. _____	

Write new words made from this word by adding prefixes or suffixes.

_____ _____ _____

_____ _____ _____

_____ _____ _____

_____ _____ _____

ANOTHER WORD FOR IT

Good writers are constantly looking for new and different words to use to make their writing more interesting.

Here are 20 words that can be used in writing to replace the verb *look.*

gaze	study	stare	perceive
see	seek	examine	discover
glance	peek	gape	notice
watch	peep	inspect	peer
survey	glimpse	observe	eye

Use your thesaurus to find 7 or more words that could be used to replace each of the following words.

<u>happy</u> (adjective)   <u>scared</u> (adjective)   <u>bad</u> (adjective)

1. _____   _____   _____
2. _____   _____   _____
3. _____   _____   _____
4. _____   _____   _____
5. _____   _____   _____
6. _____   _____   _____
7. _____   _____   _____

<u>beautiful</u> (adjective)   <u>neat</u> (adjective)   <u>show</u> (verb)

1. _____   _____   _____
2. _____   _____   _____
3. _____   _____   _____
4. _____   _____   _____
5. _____   _____   _____
6. _____   _____   _____
7. _____   _____   _____

CAMPING OUT

Read this story.

Then use your dictionary or a thesaurus to find a more colorful word for each underlined word.

Rewrite the story with the more colorful words.

Add a last line to make the story more interesting.

As the sun rose, the day began to brighten. A <u>sparkling</u> dew <u>covered</u> the <u>ground</u>, and the <u>world</u> seemed to <u>glisten</u>. The few clouds in the sky looked like <u>fluffy</u> marshmallows. Birds and other animals were <u>waking up</u>, and we heard some <u>unfamiliar</u> <u>noises</u>.

We were <u>glad</u> that no one else was camping in the <u>woods</u>. We were getting ready for breakfast and the <u>long</u> morning <u>walk</u> we took each day. We folded our tents and looked forward to the <u>new</u> day.

_____

_____

_____

_____

_____

_____

_____

_____

_____

_____

_____

_____

PUNCTUATION SITUATION

Read the story below. First, write in the correct punctuation marks. Then write 3 sentences to supply a surprise ending.

What would you do if you found yourself on a strange planet and the only sign of life you saw was a rock that had   Punctuation Planet   written on it   Maybe you would look for a trail or footprints   I don't know what I would do   but one thing I do know   I would be frightened   I would want to find a friend or two or look for a way to send a message back to Earth   I would begin to look around for food   shelter   and clothing just in case no rescue came   Can you imagine being in this punctuation situation

Well   I _____

_____

_____

_____

_____

_____

_____

_____

_____

_____

_____

_____

_____

ALL ADVICE IS NOT GOOD ADVICE

Read about the fox and the goat.
Rewrite the story and make up the conversation between the fox and the goat. Use quotation marks around their actual words.

THE FOX AND THE GOAT

A fox fell into a well and was unable to escape. He was trying to solve his problem when a thirsty goat came along.

The goat asked if the water was good and whether there was enough for him.

The fox replied that there was plenty of delicious water and invited the goat into the well to quench his thirst.

The goat couldn't resist and leaped into the well. The fox climbed up on the goat's horns and escaped. When he got out, he called down to the trapped goat.

He told the goat that if he had half as much of a brain as he had a beard, he would have looked before he leaped.

_____

_____

_____

_____

_____

_____

_____

_____

_____

_____

SPROUT A THOUGHT

A sentence expresses a complete thought and should always make sense.

Read the sentences and phrases below.

If the words form a sentence, place the correct punctuation mark at the end, and color the spaces in the puzzle that show that number.

If the group of words forms a phrase, move on to the next line.

1. You can sprout almost any seed, bean, or grain
2. In a clear pint jar
3. The tastiest things to sprout
4. Sprouts are full of vitamins
5. Do you like sprouts with your salad
6. At a 45-degree angle
7. Cover the jar with cheesecloth
8. Seeds that float are sterile and will never sprout
9. Depending on the temperature
10. Does it take only 3 to 6 days to sprout seeds

PUNCTUATION RATING

Read each punctuation rule carefully.
Use the rating scale to show how often you use each rule.
Add up your points. If your punctuation rating is below 50,
study your punctuation rules.

	Always	Most of the time	Some of the time	Almost Never
I use a period:				
1. at the end of a declarative sentence	4	3	2	1
2. after numerals and letters in outlines	4	3	2	1
3. at the end of an imperative sentence	4	3	2	1
4. after an abbreviation or initial	4	3	2	1
I use a question mark:				
5. at the end of an interrogative sentence	4	3	2	1
I use an exclamation point:				
6. at the end of an exclamatory sentence	4	3	2	1
I use a comma:				
7. to separate items in a series	4	3	2	1
8. to separate the day of the month from the year	4	3	2	1
9. to separate a direct quotation from the the rest of the sentence	4	3	2	1
10. after the greeting in a friendly letter	4	3	2	1
I use an apostrophe:				
11. to show possession	4	3	2	1
12. in contractions	4	3	2	1
I use quotation marks:				
13. to enclose the exact words of a speaker	4	3	2	1
14. around titles of short stories, poems, and songs	4	3	2	1

POOR PETER

Read poor Peter's story and supply the missing punctuation marks.

Check your work by crossing out each punctuation symbol as you place it correctly in the story.

. . . . . . , , , , , , , , , , , , " " " " " " ? ? !

Peter awoke suddenly and sat up in bed He held his hand over his mouth to smother the scream that he felt coming His heart beat wildly and he could hardly breathe Where was that strange noise coming from The same thud thud thud then a loud clump was repeated over and over It sounded like a large body coming downstairs 3 at a time resting on the fourth step and starting over Peter knew however that there were no steps inside the house As he crept silently from his bed he thought to himself Why oh why did I insist on staying home alone on Friday the thirteenth

Just then _____

_____

_____

_____

_____

_____

_____

_____

_____

_____

_____

_____

_____

_____

_____

SUPPLY THE CAPITALS

Barbara wrote this letter to her friend Jerry.
Jerry didn't answer the letter.
Could it have been because Barbara failed to use capital letters in her letter?
Correct the letter by writing the necessary capitals over the lowercase letters.
When you have finished, turn the page upside down to find all the letters you should have used.

311 center street
plaintown, kentucky
thursday , august 2

dear jerry,

　　this has been a long, hot summer. i have been busy with several projects. last tuesday, july 31, was my birthday. karen gave me a book entitled <u>the runaway princess.</u> it was written by a famous author named gloria t. whipple who lives in santa ana, california. i heard that she was born in denmark and that she speaks french, english, and dutch. mr. thompson, our english teacher, told me about her early life.

　　i hope you will be coming to plaintown soon.

yours truly,
barbara

C,S,P,K,T,A,D,J,T,I,L,T,J,K,T,R,P,I,G,T,W,S,A,C,I,D,F,E,D,M,T,E,I,P,X,B

COLLECTORS ONLY

Good writers are usually good "word collectors," always on the lookout for exciting and unusual words to add to their speaking, reading, and writing vocabularies.

As you write this week, be a "word collector" and fill the shelves below with your "trophies."

WORDS TO LEARN AND USE IN CONVERSATION

WORDS TO LEARN TO SPELL FOR WRITING

WORDS TO LEARN THE DEFINITIONS OF FOR READING

STEP UP TO BETTER SPELLING

Good writers have to be good spellers.

Using the steps below to study new words will help to improve spelling skills.

Read the steps carefully, then copy them on the steps in the order they should be used.

- Write the word again.

- Close your eyes. Try to "see" the word as you spell it.

- Check to see if you spelled it correctly this time. If not, study it again.

- Cover the word with your hand. Write it. Raise your hand to see if you spelled it correctly. If not, close your eyes and try to "see" it again.

- Look at the word carefully. Go over each letter.

BLACKOUT

Look around the room to find 5 items that are powered by electricity.

Write the name of each item on a line below. Beside each item, write a good sentence to tell how you could replace it if there were an electrical blackout for 30 days.

1. _____ _____

   _____

   _____

2. _____ _____

   _____

   _____

3. _____ _____

   _____

   _____

4. _____ _____

   _____

   _____

5. _____ _____

   _____

   _____

SIGN LANGUAGE

Write a complete sentence to tell what you think each of these signs means.

1. _____

_____

2. _____

_____

3. _____

_____

4. _____

_____

5. _____

_____

BECKY'S FIRST DAY

The following paragraph contains run-on sentences.
Rewrite the paragraph and divide the sentences that are too long into more readable ones.
Make the paragraph smooth and flowing.
Be sure to use correct punctuation.

My cousin Becky came to visit for the first time and I wanted to give her the grand tour of my neighborhood so she could meet all my friends. We walked up and down the block and I introduced her to some people and said that we would all play together after dinner. Then I took out some of my allowance and said I would treat Becky to an ice cream cone but she preferred a popsicle instead. We arrived home in time for dinner but neither of us was hungry and we stared at our food. We sat for an hour and we couldn't eat but all the other kids were back outside and they were choosing teams for a kickball game. It looked as if another day might pass before Becky got to play with my friends.

_____

_____

_____

_____

_____

_____

_____

_____

_____

_____

_____

SENTENCE SELECTION

Read the words in the columns below.

Write 4 sentences using one word or phrase from each column.

Use all the words and phrases.

I	II	III
the good ship *Lollipop*	landed	in space
the trained astronaut	orbited	for final inspection
the earth person	reported	on a strange planet
Satellite II	awaited	an unexpected crater

1. _____

_____

2. _____

_____

3. _____

_____

4. _____

_____

OUT OF THIS WORLD

Write a complete sentence to tell what you would do in each of the following situations.

1. An interesting creature from another planet knocks on your bedroom window.

   _____

   _____

2. Suddenly the lights from the spaceship start flashing.

   _____

   _____

3. The creature asks you if you would like to take a trip to Venus.

   _____

   _____

4. You start to get dressed and can't find your shoes.

   _____

   _____

5. As you are about to be beamed up, you realize that you forgot to leave your parents a note.

   _____

   _____

6. You find yourself in a room surrounded by bright lights and hundreds of large-eyed creatures.

   _____

   _____

GIVE YOUR REASONS

Select one of the topics below and write a good paragraph to convince someone else that you are right.

Underline the topic sentence in the paragraph.

Don't forget to indent and to check your work for correct punctuation and capitalization.

1. Students should be allowed to help make all school rules.
2. When accompanied by an adult, people thirteen years old and younger should be allowed to travel on airplanes and trains free of charge.
3. Teachers should never assign homework on weekends or holidays.
4. Students should not watch TV for more than one hour on school nights.

_____

_____

_____

_____

_____

_____

_____

_____

_____

_____

_____

_____

AN EXACT EXPLANATION

Look in a magazine for a picture of an unusual animal or an animal in an unusual setting.

Cut it out and glue it in the square below.

Write 10 words that describe the picture.

Then use the back of this paper to write a paragraph to explain how the animal looks. Imagine that a person who has never seen the picture will read your paragraph. Make your description as exact as possible by using the 10 words you chose.

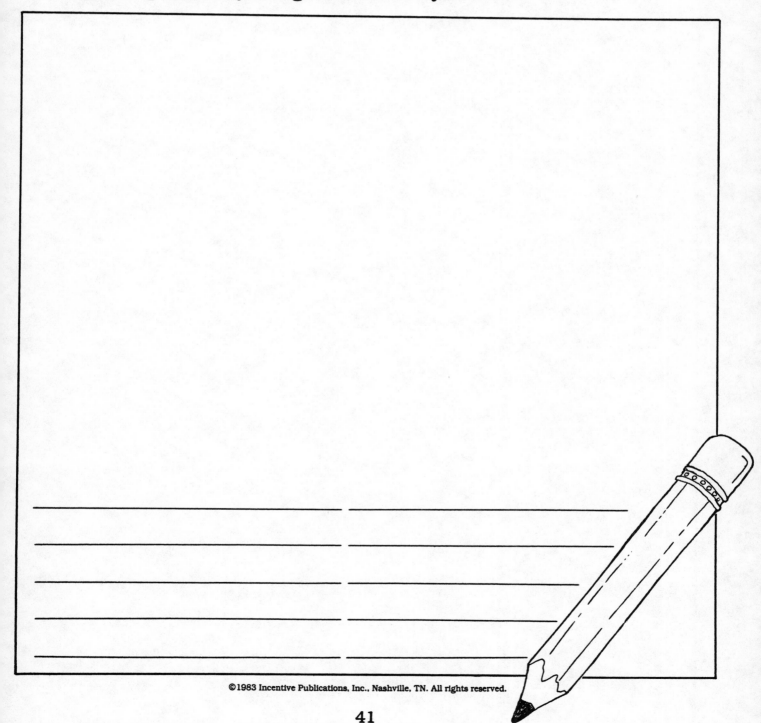

COMPOSITION AND ORIGINAL WRITING

BIOGRAPHICAL DATA

Interview an adult you find interesting.
Fill out this biographical data sheet and use the information to write the person's biography.
Remember, a biography must include *facts*, not fiction.

Name _____

Parents' names _____

Date of birth _____

Place of birth _____

Childhood (unusual events, talents, achievements) _____
_____

Teenage years (hobbies, academic interests, trips)_____
_____

Adult life (occupation, special recognition, community contributions, family) _____
_____
_____
_____

Other important facts _____
_____
_____
_____
_____
_____
_____
_____
_____

#1 BEST SELLER

The Amazing Life of Eddie B. Great

A LIFE WORTH WRITING ABOUT

Use the information gathered on the biographical data sheet to write a biography.

A *biography* must be a true account of the person's life. The writer can add interest by including the most exciting events and by using colorful and creative words and sentences.

This is a biography of _____

_____

_____

_____

_____

_____

_____

_____

_____

_____

_____

_____

_____

_____

_____

_____

_____

_____

_____

DICTIONARY TOWN

Find each of the words on the signs in Dictionary Town in your dictionary. Some signs have 2 words. You should find 14 words in all.

On the lines below, write the words and their phonetic spellings as shown in the dictionary in parenthesis beside each word.

Example: street (strēt)

1. _____   8. _____

2. _____   9. _____

3. _____   10. _____

4. _____   11. _____

5. _____   12. _____

6. _____   13. _____

7. _____   14. _____

PLANETARY PLANNING

If you could visit a planet other than Earth for one day, which of these planets would you visit? Circle your choice.

Mars
Jupiter
Pluto

Use the encyclopedia to locate information about this planet.

Write the full name of the encyclopedia set you will be using.

_____

Write the letter and the number identifying the volume in which you found the information.

Volume _____ Number _____

List 3 important facts about this planet and give the page number on which each fact was found.

1. _____

_____ Page _____

2. _____

_____ Page _____

3. _____

_____ Page _____

Use your imagination and list 3 things you might find on this planet that you could not find on Earth.

1. _____

2. _____

3. _____

PICTURES AND PROVERBS

Draw a line from each proverb to the picture that best illustrates it. Write a second sentence that you think the person in the picture might add.

_____

Let sleeping dogs lie.

_____

Two heads are better than one.

_____

_____

Money doesn't grow on trees.

Birds of a feather
flock together.

STEP-BY-STEP

Choose *one* of the following tasks.

_____ wrapping a birthday gift

_____ tying a shoe

_____ making a bed

On the lines below, write step-by-step instructions for a person to follow who has *never* performed that task.

Number each step.

After you have finished, reread your instructions. Are they clear? Have you left out anything?

_____

_____

_____

_____

_____

_____

_____

_____

_____

_____

_____

_____

_____

SCRIPT WRITER

Choose one of the following stories to rewrite as a TV serial. Divide the story and make a plan for presenting this story in 3 parts. Write the dialogue on another sheet of paper.

"Jack and the Beanstalk"
"Cinderella"
"Hansel and Gretel"

Story _____

Characters _____

_____

Plot and plan for Part I _____

_____

_____

_____

_____

Plot and plan for Part II _____

_____

_____

_____

_____

Plot and plan for Part III _____

_____

_____

_____

_____

MAKING A BIG SPLASH

This story is for you to write. Look at the pictures in all the parts. Decide which part should begin the story. Write the words for that part. Then find the second part, and write the words for that part.

Keep going until you have finished the story. Then connect the parts in order with a squiggle line so your friends can read your story.

A CHANGE OF ATTITUDE

Read the sentences carefully.

Then build an interesting story by writing the number beside each sentence to show how it should appear in the story.

☐ For that reason her black dress and Halloween hat were tattered and torn and not very presentable.

☐ So she hurriedly found a needle, thread, and some scissors.

☐ Her broomstick was getting old, and she had completely neglected to get a new sky map.

☐ The witch wardrobe catalog had not been exciting this year, and she had not ordered any new clothes.

☐ She cut and stitched, twisted and turned, and improvised in every way possible.

☐ Next she borrowed a bolt of red-and-green checked gauze from her cousin the Christmas witch.

☐ The grumpy old witch just wasn't ready for another Halloween ride.

☐ "Who ever thought of orange and black for Halloween colors anyway?" she thought. "This year I will do something different."

☐ She grabbed a star for her hat and exclaimed as she jumped on her broomstick, "It's amazing what a change of attitude can do for a grumpy witch!"

☐ Before you could say, "Trick or treat!" she had made a new hat and dress and had tied a big red bow to her broomstick.

☐ She wasn't even sure she could find her way to the village she was assigned.

☐ Besides all this, she was tired of the same old jack-o'-lanterns and kids' costumes and those boring candied apples and jelly beans.

MUSEUM MATCHUP

The pieces of this puzzle can be put together several different ways. Each way will show a different picture.

Cut out the puzzle pieces. Arrange and rearrange them in the frame below to form different pictures. After you have experimented with several arrangements, select the one you like best and paste it in place.

Give your completed picture a name. Then write a brief description of it for a museum catalog.

_____

_____

_____

_____

_____

_____

_____

_____

_____

_____

MOST IMPORTANT MEMOS

Memo is short for *memorandum.* A memo is a very short message written to give some very specific information in the fewest words possible.

Write a memo for each of the messages below. Remember, use the fewest words possible, but make sure your memo tells what, when, where, and why.

Cinderella wants to tell her stepmother that she is moving out of the house immediately, and that a messenger will come for her clothes and other possessions next Tuesday.

★ Glass Slipper Memo

From:

To:

Royal Memo

From:

To:

King Arthur wants to tell the knights of the Round Table that the next meeting to decide on new membership will be held during the third week of May.

From the Desk of:

To:

Ali Baba wants to tell Jasmine not to worry about how he is preparing to deal with the 40 thieves once they enter the courtyard.

GIFTS GALORE

Many people like to order gifts by mail.

The companies that sell the gifts mail catalogs with pictures and short descriptions of the items.

The customers look at the pictures, read the descriptions, and decide which items to buy.

Pretend that you are in charge of writing the descriptions that will convince a customer to buy each of the following items. Be sure the descriptions are brief and will grab the customer's attention.

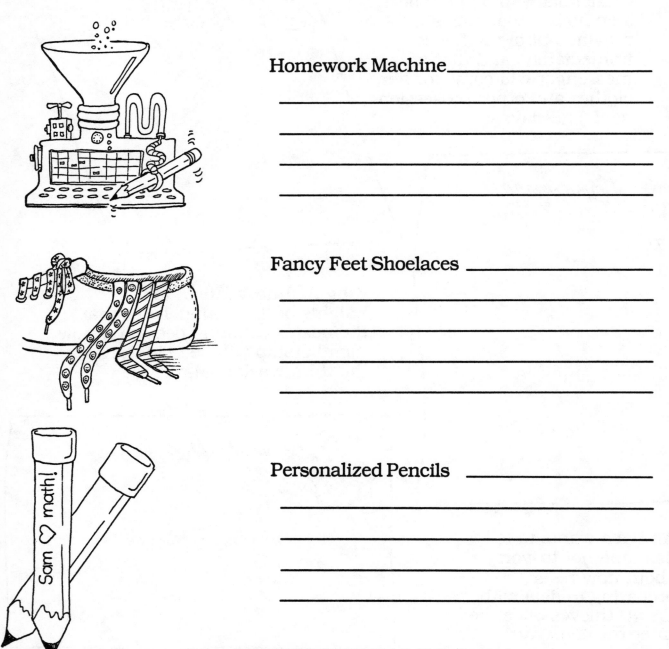

Homework Machine _____

_____

_____

_____

_____

Fancy Feet Shoelaces _____

_____

_____

_____

_____

Personalized Pencils _____

_____

_____

_____

_____

FOR SALE

Look in the classified ad section of your local newspaper for *précis* writing at its best. Since classified ads are paid for by the line, they are usually written with the fewest words possible.

Use the fewest words possible to write a classified ad to sell each of the items below.

Describe each item fully and be sure to include the price and any special "selling" features.

Snake Cage

_____

_____

_____

Hand-Painted Mug

_____

_____

_____

Humming Dog

_____

_____

_____

ON THE BOOKS

Saying the same thing in a different way is called *paraphrasing*. Usually paraphrasing is done to make something more clearly understood by using different words.

Paraphrase these laws made by early citizens of Wild Oats, U.S.A., to make them clearer and more concise.

Boots and heavy shoes are fine for streets and sidewalks, but should always be replaced with slippers by gentlemen entering the town hall or ballroom.

_____

_____

_____

People who owe large sums of money for longer than ninety to one hundred and sixty days and do not make payment of these debts as promised, shall be subject to a prison sentence or obligated to work for a specified number of days for the person to whom they owe the money.

_____

_____

_____

Spitting on the floor in public places is unsanitary and nasty and is prohibited by law and punishable according to the laws of the land.

_____

_____

_____

Borrowing another person's horse or mule for your own use without first seeking permission from the owner of the horse or mule is dishonest and despicable and will be cause for a stiff fine.

_____

_____

SEASHORE SIMILES

Similes are a way to compare two unlike things using the words *like* or *as*. In the following paragraph, underline all the similes. Complete the story by adding three sentences with similes.

The day was as clear as a bell and as warm as a wool sweater in the winter. We were walking by the seashore and there was much to see. The seagulls were huddled on the beach like a group of people waiting to see a movie, and some of them would fly off as fast as lightning. There were small tidepools that sparkled like diamonds and had tiny crabs in them. At the water's edge, we saw dozens of seashells as pretty as a picture and lots of fish darting back and forth like thieves. The dune grass waved like a flag in the breeze and was surrounded by sea oats. The seashore was certainly a peaceful place — as quiet as a mouse.

_____

_____

_____

_____

_____

_____

_____

_____

_____

_____

_____

_____

COMICAL CHARACTERS

Write a silly consonant story to fit each comical character. In each story, use as many words as possible that begin with the same letter as the character's name.

__Patchwork Pete__ Patchwork Pete from Pittsburgh puts peanuts in pans and pails. He likes pumpkin pie, pineapple, and popcorn. He punches people who poke at pigs! Pete wears pink pantaloons, drives a purple pickup, and plays piccolo in the band.

Ragged Rex _____

_____

_____

_____

Jamie Jumper _____

_____

_____

_____

Tilly Toad _____

_____

_____

_____

Careless Carolyn _____

_____

_____

THE VIEW FROM BELOW

Dolphins have been known to offer rides to people and take delight in sharing games with humans. There also have been many cases of dolphins helping humans in difficult situations, taking care not to hurt them. The dolphin family (called *Cetaceans*) has a high level of intelligence and some think this may be a reason for the caring attitude.

If a dolphin decides to offer you a ride, you should be ready to take a deep breath and hang on to the dorsal fin. It won't be easy to breathe at the fast speed that the dolphin travels, but you'll have an exciting ride!

Pretend you are swimming in the ocean and a dolphin offers you a ride. Write a story of the ride from the *dolphin's* point of view.

_____

_____

_____

_____

_____

_____

_____

_____

_____

_____

_____

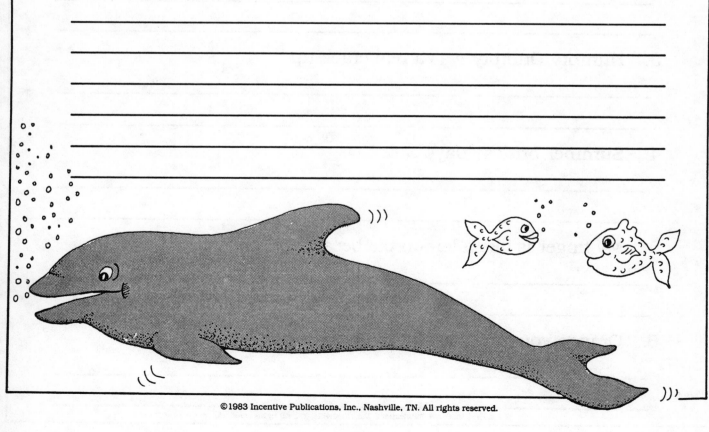

PUNNILY SPEAKING

A *pun* is the use of a word or a sound similar to a word so it suggests multiple meanings.

A pun is usually humorous.

If you have eggs for breakfast and tell the person who cooks them that they are "eggcellent," you have made a pun.

If your parents buy 3 new chairs and you say, "Three chairs for Mom and Dad," you have made a pun. You have used the "3 cheers" idea and made the remark fit the situation.

Underline the pun in each sentence.
On the lines below each sentence, explain why it is a pun.

1. Fred is the punniest kid in our class.

    _____

    _____

2. The gnomes will have their parade shortly.

    _____

    _____

3. Humpty Dumpty was a real crack-up.

    _____

    _____

4. Summer brings "days ease."

    _____

    _____

5. My finger is like a lemon pie because it has meringue on it.

    _____

    _____

6. Orange you going to Florida for vacation?

    _____

    _____

TURNAROUND ANSWERS

You are usually asked to write answers to questions. This time, you write the questions.

1. Question: _____
   Answer: Traveling clowns.

2. Question: _____
   Answer: About a hundred years ago.

3. Question: _____
   Answer: Faster than a speeding bullet.

4. Question: _____
   Answer: An animal with a long neck.

5. Question: _____
   Answer: Hearts in a spin.

6. Question: _____
   Answer: A real thirst-quencher.

7. Question: _____
   Answer: A millionaire.

8. Question: _____
   Answer: It's later than you think.

9. Question: _____
   Answer: A lawn mower.

10. Question: _____
    Answer: On a small scale.

THE LAST STORY

Just pretend that you are holding the last pencil in the world.
Think carefully before writing.
Then write what could be the world's last story.

THE LAST PENCIL IN THE WORLD

A LETTER WORTH READING

Select one of the following letters to write.
Use the most imaginative *heading*,
greeting, *body*, and *closing* that you can.

From	To
a visitor to Earth from Mars	her teacher on Mars
Cinderella	her stepmother's attorney
Mother Goose	her travel agent
the Queen of England	the President of the United States
Christopher Columbus	Queen Isabella
Romeo	Juliet

INTERESTING CHARACTERS

Look carefully at each person pictured below.

Think about what kind of person each might be. Then think about what influenced you to think this.

Give each person a name.

Under each name, write 3 characteristics which describe the person.

Write a sentence that tells what you think this person would do first if the house was on fire and all three were trapped inside.

Name _____

_____

_____

_____

_____

_____

Name _____

_____

_____

_____

_____

Name _____

_____

_____

_____

_____

_____

IT'S YOUR LIFE

An *autobiography* is the story of a person's life, written by that person.

An autobiography includes facts about time and place of birth, family, schools attended, and places lived. A good autobiography also includes things of interest such as hobbies, friends, likes, dislikes, and dreams for the future.

Write your autobiography here. Be sure to add some funny incidents, unique experiences, or "colorful" information. After all, you want everyone you know to be aware of how very special your life is.

WAY TO GO

Make each of the shapes below into a vehicle to take you to another planet.

Then complete the information sheet for each vehicle.

Name _____

Destination _____

Description _____

_____

_____

Plans for trip _____

_____

_____

Name _____

Destination _____

Description _____

_____

_____

Plans for trip _____

_____

_____

PICNIC

Write the conversation that is taking place.
Then draw a panel to show what will happen next.

AN AIR OF MYSTERY

Name the mystery character and complete her identification card.

Give her a destination and an assignment.

Write the story of her trip.

IDENTIFICATION CARD

Name _____

Address _____

_____

Age _____ Weight _____

Height _____ Color of eyes _____

Occupation _____

Destination _____

Assignment _____

_____

_____

_____

Story

_____

_____

_____

_____

_____

_____

_____

_____

_____

SPIN A TALE

Look at the picture above and write a story to tell what you think is happening.

_____

_____

_____

_____

_____

_____

_____

_____

_____

_____

_____

_____

THE TRAVELS OF TRACY AND TONY

Tell a tall tale about the travels of Tracy and Tony.
Use as many *T* words in the story as you can.

T words (Use your dictionary to find more.)

try	train	teacher
trip	tense	trembled
travelogue	twilight	triumphant
tiny	thirsty	thorough
tremendous	Thursday	trust

Tracy and Tony were terrified as they traveled timidly down the tiny tree-lined trail.

_____

_____

_____

_____

_____

_____

_____

_____

_____

_____

_____

_____

ANIMAL ANTICS

Cut 4 pictures of animals from magazines. Cut the animals apart and glue together parts from the 4 to make 2 funny animals. Draw in a background.

Name the animals and write a mystery story about an adventure the animals might have.

LUCKY, UNLUCKY THIRTEEN

Many people think that the number 13 is an unlucky number.
Other people think that it is a lucky number.
Write a complete sentence to tell what you think it is.

_____

Now use exactly 13 sentences to complete this story.
Give your lucky/unlucky story a title and a surprise ending.

_____

The darkening sky, howling wind, and driving rain seemed
appropriate for this eerie Friday the thirteenth.

_____

_____

_____

_____

_____

_____

_____

_____

_____

_____

_____

_____

_____

_____

NEWS FLASH

Read the news story carefully.
Then write 5 sentences to summarize this news bulletin for a radio broadcast.

Heavy winds and thundershowers began about 6:30 p.m. An hour and a half later, hurricane warnings were posted. It was about 8:30 when residents of the island knew they were in for some serious weather problems. By this time the waves were beating against the pier with enough force to send heavy boards and railings into the air. The wind whipped against the lighthouse and ripped off the shutters and destroyed most of the roof. Two fishing boats were overturned near the shore. Fortunately all 6 men in the 2 boats were able to swim ashore and pull in their overturned boats. The smaller boat, however, was a total loss. One of the fishermen in this boat was knocked unconscious and was rescued by his friend, who later collapsed from exhaustion. Both men were hospitalized. Several houses were damaged severely, and a number of the island's largest trees were uprooted. This is the worst hurricane to be recorded in the island's history.

ON STAGE

Spread your hand wide open and draw around the fingers.

Add features, clothing, and any other details to make each of the 5 fingers into a make-believe creature.

On another sheet of paper, write a play featuring the 5 characters.

Be sure that your play has an interesting title, setting, plot, and climax.

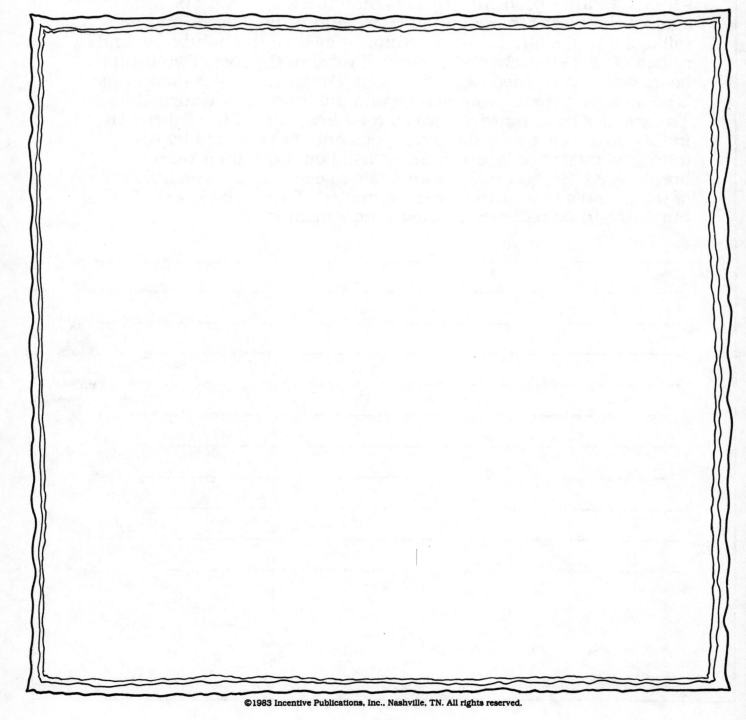

KALEIDOSCOPE

Use your crayons to make this beautiful kaleidoscope even more beautiful. Try to use every crayon in your box at least once.

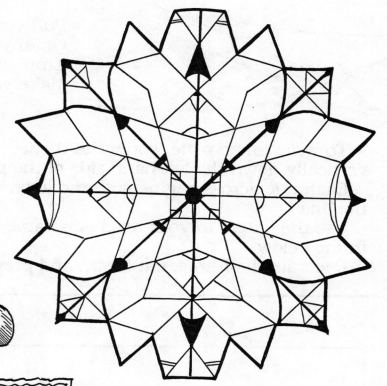

CRAYON

Write a cinquain to express the beauty of your colored design. Remember, in a cinquain:

- Line 1 is a one-word subject or idea.
- Line 2 is two adjectives describing the subject.
- Line 3 is three verbs showing action related to the subject.
- Line 4 is four words giving your personal reaction to the subject.
- Line 5 is a one-word synonym for the subject.

YOU'RE A POET, AND YOU KNOW IT!

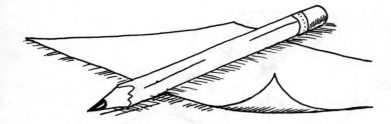

Pull your thoughts together
On anything you choose;
Employ your sense of rhythm . . .
Make your words amuse.

To write an acrostic, you write the word that the poem is about vertically down the left-hand side of the paper.

Each line across begins with the letter that is at the beginning of the line.

Use the letters in your teacher's name to write an acrostic in the frame below.

Decorate the frame, cut it out, and present it to the teacher.